all that the
PROPHETS
have spoken

WorkBook

Published by GoodSeed® International

ALL THAT THE PROPHETS HAVE SPOKEN—WORKBOOK
Edition 2

Copyright © 2011 by GOODSEED® International

Email: info@goodseed.com

GOODSEED® International
P.O. Box 3704
Olds, AB T4H 1P5
Canada

ISBN   978-1-890082-81-9

Printed in USA   201110-119-2000

I would like to express appreciation to Meredith DeRidder for pioneering this WorkBook, to my daughter, Naomi for taking it the next great leap forward, and to my wife, Janice and my brother, David for giving it the final polish.

WHAT THE BIBLE SAYS ABOUT GOD:

Blessed are they who ... seek him with all their heart.

PSALM 119:2 NIV

... he who comes to God must believe that He is, and that He is a rewarder of those who diligently seek Him.

HEBREWS 11:6 NKJV

❖ v

CONTENTS REVIEW QUESTIONS

TAKE TIME TO READ THIS ...

1. This WORKBOOK is intended to be used with the book entitled, ALL THAT THE PROPHETS HAVE SPOKEN. ALL THAT THE PROPHETS includes approximately 1200 Scripture verses quoted with accompanying commentary. Although it's your study guide, it reads like a storybook, not a textbook. If you don't have this book, see the back page of this WORKBOOK to order a copy. The WORKBOOK questions and answers are keyed to this book.

2. Learn for the sake of *knowing* for yourself. The point of this book is to study the main theme of God's Word. Whether you believe it or not is up to you. We would encourage you to reserve your final conclusions until the end of your study.

3. Get the big picture first. Don't impede the study's momentum. Unless it is a question needed to clarify subject material being studied, write down your query and save it till the end. Once you have the big picture in mind, you can go back and fill in the details by getting your questions answered.

4. Learn one section at a time in the sequence it is written. This is not the type of study where you can jump around from one lesson to another. It is important that you read each chapter section in ALL THAT THE PROPHETS and answer the questions in this WORKBOOK first, **before** you move on to the next section. If you answer a question incorrectly, look it up on the page as indicated and briefly review the material. It will only take a minute, but it will help you immensely as you study deeper into the book.

5. If stopping and answering the questions in this WorkBook seems to disrupt the flow of the story in your mind, then set it aside and just read ALL THAT THE PROPHETS HAVE SPOKEN.

6. Make sure you complete the study. To make a final judgment about the primary message of Scripture before finishing the study, entails a high risk of drawing wrong conclusions.

7. The questions in this WORKBOOK should **not** be viewed as an exam or test. They are *review questions* only—to help you make sure you have a grip on the key points. Don't be insulted if you find a question too easy—it means you understand the material. Others may find it difficult. In a number of instances, more than one answer is right. Mark all that are correct. For *fill-in-the-blank* questions, the number of letters in the word are indicated by the line spaces.

8. The content under the label FOR FURTHER CONSIDERATION not only reinforces what you have learned, but helps develop Bible navigation skills.

Now open ALL THAT THE PROPHETS HAVE SPOKEN, read the Preface, and then begin with Chapter One. Enjoy your study!

CHAPTER ONE

REVIEW QUESTIONS

1 PROLOGUE

There are no questions on this section.

2 GETTING THINGS STRAIGHT

1. The Scripture has been a best-seller for centuries. It has some very profound things to say about both life and death.
   ❏ True   ❏ False

2. In many ways, the Word of God is like a puzzle—that is, to understand it accurately, the scriptural pieces must be put together in the right way.
   ❏ True   ❏ False

3. Important keys for gaining an understanding of Scripture include:
   A. giving priority to learning the most important information first.
   B. starting at the beginning and then studying it in the order events are said to have happened.
   C. learning the simple concepts first, then moving on to the more complex—building on previously gained knowledge.
   D. sticking to one subject at a time.
   E. All of the above.

3 A UNIQUE BOOK

1. The Scripture is unique in the sense that it speaks with harmony and continuity, in spite of the fact that (Mark three):
   A. it was written in 14 different languages.
   B. it was written over a period of 1500 years.
   C. those who wrote did so from three different continents.
   D. those writing came from different walks of life.

2. By far the most unique thing about the Scripture is that it claims to be God's own words.
   ❏ True   ❏ False

3. Who is the ultimate source of every book in Scripture?

    A. A single human prophet

    B. God himself

    C. The Scriptures do not say

4. God and his words are inseparable, which is one reason Scripture is often referred to as:

    A. God's Word.   B. a sacred book.

5. The Scripture says that God guided the prophets in such a way that what was recorded was precisely what he wanted written. As necessary, they could add related thoughts.

    ❑ True   ❑ False

6. We have ample reason to be assured that the Scripture we have today is _____ what the prophets wrote centuries ago.

    A. radically different than

    B. somewhat similar in the essentials to

    C. essentially the same as

7. Translations of *The Law, Writings and the Prophets* use manuscripts that we can still read today—manuscripts dating back to 100 years before the birth of Christ.

    ❑ True   ❑ False

8. The prophets themselves said that God was unable to preserve his written Word in a way that it could still be trusted today.

    ❑ True   ❑ False

9. God is great and consistent with his character, he has preserved his Word in a marvelous way. The Scripture says that *"not the smallest letter or stroke shall pass from the Law until all is accomplished."* (MATTHEW 5:18 NASB)

    ❑ True   ❑ False

10. In reference to God, the Scripture makes a very significant claim. It claims:

    A. to express man's ideas about who God is and his will for mankind.

    B. to be God's message to mankind.

CHAPTER TWO

REVIEW QUESTIONS

1 IN THE BEGINNING GOD

1. God is so great that he created himself in eternity past.
   ❑ True   ❑ False

2. The Scripture says that God is _____, existing from everlasting past to everlasting future.

3. According to God's Word, what does God need to exist?
   A. The basic essentials of all life
   B. Eternal matter
   C. Nothing

4. God has many names that describe the greatness of his character. One of these is the name ____ _____, indicative that he is the *self-existent one.*

5. God's personal name is YAHWEH, having reference to his self-existence. This name is frequently translated as LORD, a reminder that there is no one greater.
   ❑ True   ❑ False

6. The term *The Most High* is indicative that there are very few like him. As a great God, he is a ruler over this domain.
   ❑ True   ❑ False

7. God's Word clearly and emphatically states that there _____
   A. is only one God.   B. are three gods.   C. are many gods.

8. The Scripture declares that another aspect of God's greatness is that he is invisible. He is _____.
   A. a force of nature
   B. the only eternal spirit—living from everlasting past to everlasting future

2 ANGELS, HOSTS AND STARS

1. The Word of God indicates that angels are (Mark two):
   A. innumerable.   B. invisible.   C. equal to God.

2. Angelic beings were created to serve God.
   ❏ True   ❏ False

3. Circle the words that most correctly communicate God's relationship with his created beings.

   He who _____ the paddle, also _____ the paddle.

creates	fixes
buys	owns
breaks	sells

4. When God created Lucifer (Mark two),
   A. he made him blameless—without fault.
   B. he was no different than other angels.
   C. he was given special responsibilities.

5. The Scriptures state that because God is great, he is worthy of:
   A. no praise.   B. some praise.   C. all praise.

6. The word *worship* means to declare a person's [*wealth* / *worth*].

CHAPTER THREE

REVIEW QUESTIONS

1 HEAVEN AND EARTH

1. "Genesis," the first book of the Bible, means *beginnings*.
   ❏ True   ❏ False

2. According to Genesis, God created everything we see and don't see. He created (Mark two):
   A. using angels.   C. out of nothing.
   B. simply by speaking.   D. using pre-existing materials.

3. God is great. He holds unlimited power in the universe not equalled by any other being.
   ❏ True   ❏ False

4. The Word teaches that God knows and understands everything but is limited in what he can do.
   ❑ True   ❑ False

5. The Scripture maintains that only God possesses a triad of attributes. He is great because he alone is *all-knowing, all-powerful* and *present everywhere at the same time.*
   ❑ True   ❑ False

2 IT WAS GOOD

1. The Word states that it took God nine days to create the world.
   ❑ True   ❑ False

2. The Scriptures indicate that the world, as originally created, was different from what we now know.
   ❑ True   ❑ False

3. The whole universe functions according to precise rules, revealing that God is a God of [*chance / order*].

4. Almost instinctively, we treat these natural laws with great respect because we understand that *whenever you have a law, you also have a consequence.*
   ❑ True   ❑ False

5. The Scripture says that, *"God saw that it was good."* (GENESIS 1:25 NASB) In other words, everything He made was (Mark all that are correct):
   A. perfect.   B. flawless.   C. without fault.

6. God's creation was perfect because perfection is part of being truly great. Two other words that describe this aspect of the Lord's pure nature are _____ and _____, both meaning *without blemish.*
   A. holy, righteous   B. good, decent   C. kind, helpful

7. God created the rich variety we see and experience for our enjoyment. God is a God who is truly _____ and _____.

   | holy | loving | righteous | caring |

3 MAN AND WOMAN

1. The Scripture says that man was created in the image of God. This means that we are exact duplicates of the LORD with all of his attributes.
   ❑ True   ❑ False

2. Which of the following statements is true?
   A. Man came alive spontaneously—without any outside cause.
   B. An angel gave life to man.
   C. God breathed life into man.

3. God had to ask Adam and Eve's permission before taking any action that would affect them.
   ❑ True   ❑ False

4. God commanded Adam and Eve not to:
   A. eat of the tree of life.
   B. eat of the tree of the knowledge of good and evil.
   C. eat from any tree in the garden.

5. The ability to [choose / walk] is what distinguishes man from a robot. It makes a relationship genuine. It is what gives meaning and depth to the word [laughter / obey].

6. The Word of God declares that mankind was created to reflect God's greatness—to honour Him as a son honours his father.
   ❑ True   ❑ False

7. The Scriptures are clear that God was not an aloof, distant Creator—he was Adam and Eve's friend.
   ❑ True   ❑ False

8. God's Word teaches us that only perfect people can live in the presence of a perfect God.
   ❑ True   ❑ False

CHAPTER FOUR

REVIEW QUESTIONS

1 SATAN

1. Lucifer's rebellion was driven by his [anger / pride], which God hates.

2. To God, a proud heart is a self-centered form of _____.
   A. love   B. respect   C. sin

3. Because of God's holy nature, he cannot tolerate __ __ __ in his presence.

4. Lucifer became known by other names—names that reveal aspects of his character. Match two meanings with each name. See page 50 if you have trouble.

    A. Devil   a. adversary

                                 b. false accuser

    B. Satan   c. slanderer

                                 d. enemy

2 HAS GOD SAID?

1. The Word of God tells us that Satan:

    A. is the great deceiver, the father of lies.

    B. is a harmless jokester.

    C. is a jinn.

    D. is a figment of one's imagination.

2. Satan first twisted God's word to cause Eve to doubt God, then he outright _____ it.

    A. ignored   B. denied   C. approved

3. A broken law has consequences. The Scripture teaches us that sin's effects are very costly.

    ❑ True   ❑ False

4. Adam and Eve sewed fig leaf clothing for themselves and hid from God because they were experiencing an uncomfortable new feeling called [guilt / defeat].

5. We do not need to live in fear of the spirit world if we listen to God, because he is more powerful than all the evil spirits and black magic combined.

    ❑ True   ❑ False

6. Adam and Eve had a __ __ __ __ __ __, to obey or not obey. God considers all disobedience, even what appears seemingly small, to be __ __ __.

7. Though Adam and Eve's sin hurt their relationship with God, it did not result in any permanent consequences or repercussions.

    ❑ True   ❑ False

8. According to the Scripture, God considered Adam and Eve's disobedience to be an innocent mistake—a misunderstanding.

    ❑ True   ❑ False

3 Where Are You?

1. The Lord wanted Adam and Eve to sort out in their minds precisely what had happened. *They had disobeyed Him! They had trusted Satan instead of God.*
   ❑ True   ❑ False

2. Adam and Eve (Mark two):
   A. were unwilling to accept responsibility for their sin.
   B. admitted that they had freely followed Satan.
   C. pointed the finger of blame at others for their sin.

3. Adam and Eve's actions affected:
   A. no one but themselves.   B. the whole human race.

4. The Word of God says that a male child was promised to come through the future offspring of Eve. This male child would free mankind from the consequences of sin. He would be known as *The Promised Deliverer.*
   ❑ True   ❑ False

5. The Scripture also states that Satan would temporarily wound the child, but the child would _____ Satan.
   A. fatally crush   B. seriously injure   C. help

6. This promise of a *Deliverer* added another name to the list of terms that reveal God's character. He would be known as *the one who saves* or *The Saviour.*
   ❑ True   ❑ False

7. Because of Adam and Eve's sin, nothing remained perfect. The earth and everything in it suffered from the effects of a:
   A. drought.   B. curse.   C. flood.

8. Just as defying the law of gravity brings broken bones, so violating God's word has ramifications. The most bitter consequence of sin is [*death / failure*].

4 Death

1. In Scripture, death implies some sort of *separation.* It may also mean annihilation or non-existence.
   ❑ True   ❑ False

2. According to the Word of God, sin has an inescapable consequence: "The ___ ___ ___ ___ ___ of sin is death ..." (Romans 6:23 NKJV)

3. Match the following:

___ A. Death of the Body   1. Separation of man's spirit from God

___ B. Death to a Relationship   2. Separation of man's spirit from God forever

___ C. Death to a Future Joy   3. Separation of man's spirit from his body

4. God, being perfect, cannot allow sin in his presence. Habakkuk 1:13 (NIV) says he is *"too pure to look on evil; [he] cannot tolerate wrong."*
   ❑ True   ❑ False

5. The _____ of _____ is a place of unending punishment that God created specifically for Satan and his followers.

6. Sinful man will experience the same punishment as Satan. The Word of God calls this the _____ death, probably because it occurs after physical death.

7. According to the Word of God, children are born with a sin nature. They do not need to be taught how to sin.
   ❑ True   ❑ False

CHAPTER FIVE

REVIEW QUESTIONS

1 A PARADOX

1. Just as God established physical laws to govern the universe, so there are spiritual [*suggestions / laws*] to govern the relationship between God and man.

2. The Scripture teaches that on the moral ledger, sin incurs a debt that can only be paid by:
   A. praying faithfully.
   B. doing one's best to be a good and humble person.
   C. giving to charity.
   D. death.
   E. fasting.

3. The Word of God states that *"the soul who sins shall die."*
   ❑ True   ❑ False

4. Man faces a problem that has two facets, like opposite sides of the same coin.

   ❖ We have something we don't want: a [*morality* / *sin*] problem with all its consequences.

   ❖ We need something we don't have: a [*goodness* / *perfection*] that allows us to live in God's presence.

5. The Scripture says that God is *just* which means that, as a perfect judge, he is always fair and impartial.
   ❑ True   ❑ False

6. God revealed a type of love when he created the world, a care and concern. But then, because man deserved it, God unveiled a deeper love. This love is often referred to using the words *grace* and *mercy*.
   ❑ True   ❑ False

7. God judges [*all* / *most* / *the worst*] of our sin, whether here during life on earth or after physical death.

8. God provided a way for man's sin-debt to be paid in order that man may escape the eternal consequences of the death penalty. God did this because:
   A. he loves those he created.
   B. Satan demands it.
   C. man deserves it.

9. God's Word declares that the same pride that caused Satan to rebel is what will keep us from coming to God for help. The Lord can only help man escape the penalty of death when man:
   A. is content with who he is.
   B. finds fulfillment in life.
   C. humbles himself and seeks God's help.
   D. helps others.

2 ATONEMENT

1. Adam and Eve could do nothing, outwardly or inwardly, to [*remove* / *forget*] their sin problem.

2. According to the Word of God, __ __ __ __ __ __ is the consequence of sin.

3. The first of Adam and Eve's children, Cain and Abel, were born sinless.
   ❑ True   ❑ False

4. The Scriptures say, *"Without the* _____,
   there is no forgiveness." (HEBREWS 9:22 NASB)
   A. washing with water
   B. shedding of blood
   C. shedding of tears

5. Based on certain future events, God said that he would accept an animal's death in man's place—as man's [*payment / substitute*].

6. The shed blood would provide an atonement-covering by which (Mark two):
   A. God no longer saw man's sin.
   B. Satan would be appeased.
   C. man could now find acceptance with God.

7. Cain's offering was not acceptable because (Mark three):
   A. he held back his best garden produce.
   B. he did not have confidence in God's instructions as being trustworthy.
   C. he did not come to God in God's way.
   D. his sacrifice could not shed blood.

8. Cain was angry, yet God was gracious and explained to him that if he came the same way his brother had come, he too would be [*accepted / excused*].

9. The Scripture declares that Heaven (Mark three):
   A. is a place for believing men and women.
   B. is an imaginary place.
   C. may or may not exist; we will have to wait and see.
   D. is a place where man's unique relationship with God will be restored.
   E. is a place without pain, tears or death.

3 THE PROPHET ENOCH

1. Enoch was a godly man who believed that only the Lord could save him from the consequences of sin.
   ❑ True   ❑ False

2. To come to God, one must (Mark two):
    A. believe that he exists.
    B. work hard to be a good person.
    C. believe that God will provide a way to have a friendship with him again.

4 THE PROPHET NOAH

1. Though the people of Noah's day disregarded the Lord, God
    _____ their sin. God is grieved by sin.
    A. was unable to do anything about
    B. did not overlook
    C. was not concerned by

2. Man may have had a life that excluded God, but God still held man accountable for sin.
    ❏ True   ❏ False

3. The prophet Noah was different from the other people of his day (Mark two):
    A. because he was a sinner.
    B. because he was a righteous man.
    C. because he trusted God.

4. The Scripture indicates that Noah brought an animal sacrifice to God, evidence that he recognized the need to have an innocent substitute pay the [*cultural / death*] penalty for him.

5. Like man, God sometimes threatens to send judgment but doesn't deliver.
    ❏ True   ❏ False

6. Only a great, all-powerful God could create the flood circumstances.
    ❏ True   ❏ False

5 BABEL

1. Man wanted to build a tower to bring honour to:
    A. God.   B. the first man, Adam.   C. himself.

2. It is right to exalt ourselves because we are truly deserving.
    ❏ True   ❏ False

3. A definition for the word _ _ _ _ _ _ _ _ is this: *man's efforts to reach God.*

4. The Word of God describes mankind as (Mark two):
   A. being in a spiritual wilderness.
   B. lost—unable to find a way back to a right relationship with God.
   C. unable to ever have a friendship with the Lord.

5. In contrast to man's religious efforts, the Scripture teaches that the only true way to be made acceptable to God was provided by the Lord himself in his compassion and mercy.
   ❑ True   ❑ False

6. God scattered man throughout the world because they refused to heed his commands and follow him.
   ❑ True   ❑ False

CHAPTER SIX

REVIEW QUESTIONS

1 THE PROPHET JOB

1. Job longed for a mediator who could approach God on his behalf and plead for mercy for Job.
   ❑ True   ❑ False

2. Job learned that the only way to be *"righteous before God"* was to:
   A. work hard at doing good things to please God.
   B. pray and hope that God would accept him.
   C. trust God to provide him with the perfection needed to be in his holy presence.

2 THE PROPHET ABRAHAM

1. Through the promises God gave to Abram (Abraham), God was telling Abram that one of his descendants would be THE SAVIOUR—THE PROMISED DELIVERER.
   ❑ True   ❑ False

2. Independent of God Abram (Abraham) found it impossible to gain *a righteousness <u>equal</u> to God's righteousness.*
   ❑ True   ❑ False

3. Cross out the incorrect answers: God said that because Abram (Abraham) [*respected / believed*] God, righteousness was [*credited to / debited from*] Abram's account, more than offsetting his sin-debt.

3 GENUINE BELIEF

1. Genuine faith is built on:
    A. facts.
    B. the way you feel.
    C. what one's predecessors believed.

2. The meaningfulness of one's faith is determined not by the amount of faith you exercise but rather in whom you are placing your trust and confidence.
    ❏ True ❏ False

3. Abram's (Abraham's) obedience was an attempt to prove to God and to others the genuineness of his faith.
    ❏ True ❏ False

4 HAGAR AND ISHMAEL

1. God told Abram (Abraham) to have a child by Hagar.
    ❏ True ❏ False

2. Though God said he would bless Ishmael and make his descendants into a great nation, he did not change his promise to Abraham that a child would be born to Sarah. His name would be Isaac.
    ❏ True ❏ False

3. God says he will honour faith *"the size of a mustard seed."* In other words, what counts is not the amount of faith you have, but in whom you are placing your trust and confidence.
    ❏ True ❏ False

5 ISHMAEL AND ISAAC

1. God kept his promise of a son to Abraham and Sarah.
    ❏ True ❏ False

2. God promised Hagar that he would make Ishmael the father of a great nation. Today, many Arab countries trace their lineage directly back to this individual.
    ❏ True ❏ False

6 THE PROVIDER

1. Though Isaac was the son through whom THE PROMISED DELIVERER was to come, Abraham obeyed the Lord because he was convinced that God could choose to raise Isaac from the dead.

   ❑ True   ❑ False

2. Even though God had intervened and told Abraham not to kill Isaac, there still was a death in his place. God provided a _____. It was God's idea.

3. God was giving Abraham another lesson about his character. God tested Abraham by commanding him to take his only son and sacrifice him on an altar to show him:

   A. that He could be appeased through child sacrifice.

   B. that He was an angry God.

   C. truths concerning *judgment, faith* and *deliverance through a substitute.*

4. Match the best parallel sentences below.

   ___ A. Just as Isaac was under God's direct order to *die,*

   ___ B. God did *intervene.*

   ___ C. An innocent *animal* died

   ___ D. Just as Abel had offered a sacrifice to die in *his place,*

   ___ E. Just as God viewed Abel's sacrifice as *acceptable,*

   1. God provided a *substitute.*

   2. so God saw fit to provide a ram as an *acceptable* sacrifice in Isaac's place.

   3. so all mankind is under the sentence of *death.*

   4. so the ram had died in *Isaac's place.*

   5. in *man's* place.

5. In Scripture, this story is a vivid illustration of two people coming to God in God's way, believing that His Word is true.

   ❑ True   ❑ False

CHAPTER SEVEN

REVIEW QUESTIONS

1 JACOB AND JUDAH

1. Isaac had two sons, Esau and Jacob. Esau was like Cain—living life according to his own ideas, but Jacob was looked upon as righteous because he came to God by faith,
    A. offering a blood sacrifice as an atonement-covering for his sin.
    B. praying daily.
    C. being a good, hard-working man.

2. God renewed His pledge to Abraham and Isaac through Jacob, saying that through Jacob's offspring would come THE PROMISED
_ _ _ _ _ _ _ _ .

2 THE PROPHET MOSES

1. Forty years after Moses fled Egypt for murdering an Egyptian, God spoke to him from a flaming bush. As Moses approached the bush, God told Moses to remove his shoes because:
    A. culturally it was the appropriate thing to do.
    B. Moses was standing on holy ground.

2. God told Moses to tell the Israelites that it was _____, the self-existent one, who had sent him to them.
    A. The Almighty God   B. The Most High   C. I AM

3 PHARAOH AND THE PASSOVER

1. God taught both the Israelites and the Egyptians that (Mark two):
    A. he delivers those who trust Him.
    B. he alone is God.
    C. only Israelites could escape God's punishment.

2. God extends love and mercy to those who come to God in God's _ _ _.

3. Because God is compassionate, it was acceptable to ignore a few of the commands concerning the Passover as long as one had the right motive.
    ❑ True   ❑ False

4. If an Egyptian followed all of God's instructions concerning the Passover, because he believed that the Lord was the only true God, the Lord would then also *pass over* his house.
    ❑ True   ❑ False

5. The firstborn lived, but only because an innocent lamb died. The lamb became the firstborn's substitute.
    ❑ True   ❑ False

6. Match the parallel sentences below having to do with the concept of substitution.

___ A. God had accepted Abel   1. the ram died *in Isaac's place.*

___ B. When Abraham offered Isaac as a sacrifice,   2. the lamb died *in the place of the firstborn.*

___ C. With the Passover,   3. because an animal had died *in his place.*

CHAPTER EIGHT

REVIEW QUESTIONS

1 BREAD, QUAIL AND WATER

1. The Israelites were content with the Lord's leading.
    ❑ True   ❑ False

2. God told Moses to tell the people to gather only as much bread as they could eat that day. There would be more the next day. God was teaching them that His Word was:
    A. to be trusted only when times were good.
    B. true and was always to be trusted.
    C. something important for them to consider.

3. Mankind does not deserve God's loving care, yet God provides for man in spite of his sin. This undeserved love is called *grace.*
    ❑ True   ❑ False

2 TEN RULES

1. God directed Moses to put a boundary line around the mountain:
    A. to protect people from falling rocks.
    B. to show the Israelites where God lived.
    C. to illustrate the separation that exists between a holy God and sinful man.

2. God told the Israelites that if anything was more important than Him in their lives, then they had broken the first rule.
   ❏ True   ❏ False

3. The Scripture declares that God does not want people worshipping idols or any other gods because:
   A. no one knows what He looks like.
   B. only God is worthy of worship.
   C. they do not resemble God.

4. Because of who God is, even his name should not be used flippantly or irreverently.
   ❏ True   ❏ False

5. The Word of God likens certain types of anger to _____.

   | murder   temper tantrums   disrespect   stress |

6. God not only knows our outward actions but also our innermost thoughts.
   ❏ True   ❏ False

7. Stealing, cheating and lying—in whatever form—are never right.
   A. True. These are totally contrary to God's character.
   B. False. Sometimes our well-being or duty requires us to bend the rules.

8. Anyone who is deceitful or dishonest is following Satan's agenda because Satan is the father of __ __ __ __.

9. Down through the years, God's expectations for mankind have changed dramatically.
   ❏ True   ❏ False

10. The Ten Rules made man aware of what the Lord considered to be sin.
    ❏ True   ❏ False

3 The Courtroom

1. In order to be accepted by God, the Scripture says that man must obey how many of the commandments?
   A. Any four, completely and perfectly
   B. The first eight (the last two are discretionary)
   C. All ten

2. God holds man accountable for all of his sin, even the sin of which he is not aware.
   ❑ True   ❑ False

3. If one tries hard enough, it is possible to obey all of God's commands consistently and perfectly.
   ❑ True   ❑ False

4. The Ten Commandments have two main objectives (Mark two):
   A. to silence those who say their lives are good enough to be accepted by God.
   B. to show mankind that we are indeed law-breakers.
   C. to give mankind a list of rules to keep in order to please God.

5. Just as a mirror exposes the dirt, so the Ten Rules expose a person's __ __ __.

6. God gave the Law so *"that through the commandment sin would become* _____ *sinful."* (ROMANS 7:13 NASB)
   A. *reasonably*   B. *utterly*   C. *somewhat*

7. The Scripture teaches that all people are sinful from the time of:
   A. conception.   B. birth.   C. their first choice to sin.

8. God directed the Israelites to be *holy*, a word that has to do with God's _____ character.
   A. aloof   B. critical   C. perfect

9. The notion that a person's good living and thinking can outweigh his bad, and therefore merit God's acceptance, is totally foreign to God's Word.
   ❑ True   ❑ False

CHAPTER NINE

REVIEW QUESTIONS

1 THE TENT OF MEETING

1. The Word states that the first step in approaching God is for man to recognize that he is a _____ sinner.
   A. worthy   B. helpless   C. hopeful   D. capable

2. The Israelites were to build a sanctuary. This was (Mark two):
   A. a special place called the Tabernacle.
   B. the same as today's religious sites.
   C. necessary because God needed a house.
   D. an elaborate visual aid created by the Lord.

3. When the Israelites built the Tabernacle, they were allowed to build it according to their own wishes.
   ❑ True   ❑ False

4. The Sanctuary was divided into two sections: one-third of the structure formed the *Holy of Holies* and the other two-thirds, the *Holy Place*. What separated the two rooms?
   A. A large door
   B. A thick curtain or veil
   C. Eight gold posts

5. With the Tabernacle completed, the cloud that led the Israelites moved into position over the Holy of Holies, signifying God's presence in the midst of his people.
   ❑ True   ❑ False

6. After entering the one and only gate, the first step to approaching God was to bow and worship the Lord.
   ❑ True   ❑ False

7. The [*hand / arm*] on the [*body / head*] symbolized the individual's sin and guilt being moved from the man onto the animal. Because the animal now carried the man's sin, it had to [*suffer / die*]. Death is the penalty for sin. It was a case of the innocent dying in the place of the guilty—as a [*substitute / advocate*]. The Word says that God [*accepted / rejected*] the sacrifice on his behalf.

8. Because death is the penalty for sin, the sacrifice pictured:
   A. God's desire for blood offerings.
   B. Satan being appeased.
   C. what was necessary for sin to be forgiven.

9. The blood of animals could not permanently cancel man's sin-debt since the life of an animal is not equal in value to the life of a human being. The Scriptures teach us that *"it is impossible for the blood of bulls and goats to take away sins."* (HEBREWS 10:4 ESV)
   ❑ True   ❑ False

10. The Scripture declares that only the High Priest was allowed to enter the Holy of Holies. He did so only once a year and never without [*food / blood*] which he offered on the Atonement Cover. This was done on the [*Passover / Day of Atonement*].

2 UNBELIEF

1. As the Israelites learned more about the Lord, they also were more _____ for those things they knew.

   | worthy | accountable | esteemed |

2. God may delay judgment on sin for a period of time, but eventually he judges all sin.
   ❑ True   ❑ False

3. God's purpose in sending judgment is to show the world that he can do whatever he chooses to do.
   ❑ True   ❑ False

4. When the Scripture uses the word *repent*, it means:
   A. to weep and feel sorry.
   B. to promise to live better.
   C. a change of mind.

5. Only during this life on earth can people repent and be heard by God.
   ❑ True   ❑ False

6. The Word of God states that the *"wages of sin is* _____*."*

3 JUDGES, KINGS AND PROPHETS

1. The Scripture teaches that because all roads—all beliefs— ultimately lead to the same God, the important thing is simply to trust in God.
   ❑ True   ❑ False

2. Unlike many of the other kings who ruled over Israel, King David trusted God. David called the Lord, "my _____."
   A. Inspiration   B. Saviour

3. God sent prophets who (Mark two):
   A. warned Israel that the LORD would judge them for their self-centeredness.
   B. were popular with the people because they were telling them what they wished to hear.
   C. gave specific information about the coming DELIVERER.

4. A group of Jewish religious leaders were known to be strict observers of the Law. They were so concerned about keeping the Ten Rules that they created additional rules to encompass God's laws so as to be careful not to break any of God's commands. These religious zealots were called _____.
   A. Sadducees   B. Scribes   C. Pharisees

5. Throughout the centuries there were always those people who waited in eager anticipation for God to fulfill his promises. Most importantly, they were waiting for the arrival of:
   A. Caesar   B. THE PROMISED DELIVERER   C. Pharaoh

6. God knew that men would come and falsely declare themselves to be THE PROMISED DELIVERER. To insure that people could identify the false from the true, God had many different prophets write about the coming Saviour over a span of hundreds of years. The likelihood of one person fulfilling all of these prophecies is beyond reasoned probability.
   ❑ True   ❑ False

CHAPTER TEN

REVIEW QUESTIONS

1 THE ANGEL GABRIEL

1. Neither the blood of animals nor another sinful human being could remove mankind's sin debt. Man needed a perfect Saviour to step forward and rescue him from the consequences of his sin.
   ❑ True   ❑ False

2. The LORD Almighty had spoken through the prophet Malachi 400 years earlier, "I will send my messenger who will prepare the way before me!" (MALACHI 3:1 NIV) This messenger would be:
   A. John   B. Zechariah   C. Gabriel   D. Joseph

3. Since Jesus was not born of a human father, he did not have Adam's sinful nature. Rather, because God was his father (referring to his character), he was perfect, just as God is perfect. He had God's nature and would be known as the *Son of God*.
   ❑ True   ❑ False

4. The name Son of Man (Mark two):
   A. implies Jesus had a human father: Joseph was Jesus' father.
   B. emphasizes Jesus humanity: he took on human form. He was fully man—though sinless.
   C. declares Jesus' true identity: for centuries, scholars of Scripture have recognized this name as referring to *THE DELIVERER*.

5. The Bible teaches that God took Mary as his wife to be the Queen of Heaven, resulting in the birth of Jesus.
   ❑ True   ❑ False

2 THE MESSIAH

1. Just as God has names that depict his character, so *THE PROMISED DELIVERER* was given names that described his character. Match each name with its meaning.
   ___ A. Jesus   1. *God with us*
   ___ B. Immanuel   2. Greek for *Messiah*
   ___ C. Christ   3. *Deliverer* or *Saviour*
   ___ D. Messiah   4. *Anointed One*

2. Over 700 years earlier, the prophet Micah recorded that *THE PROMISED MESSIAH* (Mark two):
   A. must be born in Bethlehem Ephrathah.
   B. would be born in a royal palace.
   C. had lived from everlasting.

3. *"In the beginning was the Word ... and the Word* _____*."*
   (JOHN 1:1 NKJV)
   A. became a god   B. was God   C. was an angelic being

4. Until this time, God had been telling mankind about himself through his spoken word and written word. But then he went one step further and showed himself to mankind by becoming a man. In reality, *"The Word became flesh and made his dwelling among us ..."*
   ❑ True   ❑ False

3 AMONG THE SAGES

1. The only story recorded in Scripture of Jesus growing up is an account of his "coming of age" when he was 12 years old.
   ❑ True   ❑ False

2. Even as a boy, Jesus made a profound impression upon the scholars in the temple.
   ❑ True   ❑ False

4 THE PROPHET JOHN

1. Baptism implies:

purity   identification   washing   physical cleanliness

2. In the Scripture, *repent* means to have *"a change of mind."*
   ❑ True   ❑ False

3. John did not feel that the Pharisees and Sadducees needed baptism because they were already very religious.
   ❑ True   ❑ False

4. John identified Jesus as THE PROMISED SAVIOUR, the one who would take away the sin of the world. John called him the [*Lamb / Gift*] of God and said that Jesus had lived [*with / before*] him—eternally.

5. The Scripture reveals to us a God who is at the same time Father, Son, and Holy Spirit—three eternal and co-equal persons that comprise the one true God.
   ❑ True   ❑ False

6. It is important to recognize that our limited ability to reason cannot fit [*an infinite / a finite*] God into our [*infinite / finite*] minds.

CHAPTER ELEVEN

REVIEW QUESTIONS

1 TEMPTED

1. Although Jesus was fully God, he was also a human being with real physical needs.
   ❑ True   ❑ False

2. Satan tempted Jesus by suggesting that he turn stones into bread for nourishment. But there was a catch. To do so, Jesus would be:
   A. demonstrating that, as God the Creator, there was no one greater in the universe.
   B. compromising who he was by following Satan's orders.

3. Jesus countered each of Satan's temptations by quoting:
   A. some respected religious philosophers.
   B. his father, Joseph.
   C. Scripture, God's written Word.

4. Jesus responded to Satan's initial challenge by stating that it was more important to be concerned about one's physical needs than to worry about one's spiritual well-being.
   ❏ True   ❏ False

5. Satan loves religion and quoting the Scripture is a favorite method of deception. The Devil quoted God's Word accurately and in context when he tempted Jesus.
   ❏ True   ❏ False

6. If Jesus bowed down and worshipped Satan, he would also be serving him.
   ❏ True   ❏ False

7. The struggle between God and Satan is a balanced battle. Jesus is just as powerful as Satan.
   ❏ True   ❏ False

8. Even those who were closest to Jesus wrote that Jesus:
   A. committed no sin, nor was deceit found in his mouth.
   B. rarely exaggerated or understated when he spoke.

2 POWER AND FAME

1. Repentance is something that happens inwardly. Jesus intended to begin his rule in the heart.
   ❏ True   ❏ False

2. Jesus spoke with authority, but could not demonstrate his claims because he was no more than a man.
   ❏ True   ❏ False

3. Jesus healed many men and women of physical handicaps and diseases because (Mark three):
    A. he was trying to gain popularity and influence among the people.
    B. he felt compassion for those in need.
    C. he wanted to establish that he and his message were from Heaven.
    D. he was powerful.

For Further Consideration:

According to the culture of that day, a leper had to shout *"unclean"* whenever anyone approached. The possibility of physical contact with a leper would not only have been repulsive but unthinkable. Yet the Scripture says that Jesus reached out his hand and deliberately touched a leper (Mark 1:40-45). That touch was not necessary. Jesus healed many people from a distance. Yet think of what that touch meant to the watching crowd—to the leprous man. The event must have been electrifying! Not only was it culturally unacceptable, but according to the Law, if a man physically contacted a leper then he was ceremonially unclean. Not so with Jesus. Rather, there was the opposite effect. Jesus touched the man and the leper became clean. That touch was intentional. It was the touch of God.

3 Nicodemus

1. When Jesus told Nicodemus that he must be born again, Jesus was referring to a mystical and miraculous rebirth as an infant.
    ❑ True   ❑ False

2. Jesus told Nicodemus that if he put his faith in Jesus, he would have _ _ _ _ _ _ _ life.

3. The scriptural meaning of the word *believe* should be understood as:
    A. a simple intellectual assent.
    B. a determination to achieve the impossible.
    C. synonymous with faith and trust.
    D. an abstract, mystical acquisition of knowledge.

4. The [*amount / object*] of one's faith is of critical importance.

5. Jesus was promising eternal life, not only to Nicodemus, but to:
    A. those whose good deeds outweighed their bad.
    B. everyone who believes in him.
    C. anyone who is religious.

6. The Word of God states that man is under judgment and destined for eternal death in the Lake of Fire until he puts his trust in Jesus to deliver him.
   ❏ True   ❏ False

7. Jesus declared that there was a middle ground—a "grey zone"— between believing him and being an unbeliever.
   ❏ True   ❏ False

8. The Scripture says that you must wait until death to find out your eternal destiny.
   ❏ True   ❏ False

4 REJECTION

1. The Scripture states that *"When Jesus saw their* _____, *he said to the paralytic, 'Son, your sins are forgiven.'"* (MARK 2:5 ESV)

energy	faith	work	love

2. Jesus showed the teachers of the law that he was God by (Mark all that are correct):
   A. forgiving sin.
   B. knowing their thoughts.
   C. healing a paralyzed man.

3. Jesus could only help those who recognized their (Mark two):

helplessness	heritage	sinfulness	self-worth

4. All the disciples (apostles) were, by profession, highly trained religious leaders.
   ❏ True   ❏ False

5 THE BREAD OF LIFE

1. Jesus could see that the people only wanted him to be king so that they could get free food. Jesus (Mark two):
   A. was seeking to rule people's hearts.
   B. said that the people's goal in life should be to pursue that which would give them eternal life.
   C. immediately did another miracle to confirm his deity.

2. When the people asked Jesus what sort of work they would have to do to earn everlasting life, Jesus replied, *"This is the deed God requires—to* _____ *the one whom he sent."* (JOHN 6:29 NET)
   A. serve   B. make king   C. believe in

CHAPTER TWELVE

REVIEW QUESTIONS

1 FILTHY RAGS

1. In the parable Jesus told about the Pharisee and the tax collector, the Pharisee was relying on his own right living to make himself righteous before God.
   - ❑ True   ❑ False

2. The tax collector was conscious of the fact that he was:
   - A. a helpless sinner.
   - B. needing to do a multitude of good deeds to be acceptable before God.
   - C. a very good and righteous man.

3. Jesus tied repentance to [*humility / self-confidence*].

4. The Pharisees were relying upon which of the following to become right with God? (Mark three)
   - A. Their religious observances   C. Their Jewish birth
   - B. Their faith in God's mercy   D. Their good deeds

5. The Scripture is very clear that good works are necessary in order for a person to earn a right standing with God.
   - ❑ True   ❑ False

6. The Word of God says that all people are:
   - A. inherently good.
   - B. slaves to sin.
   - C. redeemable by good works.

7. God holds everyone accountable for the choices they make.
   - ❑ True   ❑ False

8. Our place of physical birth has [*nothing / everything*] to do with our relationship with God and our future destiny.

2 THE WAY

1. In the Scripture passage, JOHN 10:7-10, Jesus likened himself to the gate of a sheep pen.
   - ❑ True   ❑ False

2. Jesus compared those who threaten sheep to:
   A. unfit parents.
   B. false teachers—those who proclaim another way to God.
   C. domineering leaders.

3. Just as there was only one way to gain entrance into the sheep pen, the only way to escape the consequences of sin is through belief in [oneself / Jesus]

4. Jesus said he is the only [way / companion] to God. His Word is the only [truth / book]. [Eternal life / Happiness] can only be found in him.

3 THE PLAN

1. Jesus not only foretold the exact method by which he would be put to death, he also described some of the events leading up to that death.
   ❑ True   ❑ False

2. Jesus said that not only would he be killed but that on the _____ day, he would be raised back to life.
   A. first   B. second   C. third   D. fourth

3. Jesus didn't mind that Peter denied the truth of his words.
   ❑ True   ❑ False

4. Jesus' outward appearance was transformed—his face and clothing radiated like the sun. The disciples saw the same dazzling pure light of God's presence that had filled the Most Holy Place in the Tabernacle centuries before.
   ❑ True   ❑ False

4 LAZARUS

1. Martha's faith in Jesus as the Messiah was misplaced. Jesus was unable to raise her brother from the dead even if he wanted to do so.
   ❑ True   ❑ False

2. Though Martha knew Lazarus would be raised to life at the end of the world, Jesus also had the power to bring him back to life at any moment.
   ❑ True   ❑ False

3. Why did Jesus pray out loud when they rolled the stone away from the tomb?
    A. So those listening would believe that Jesus was the Promised Saviour who came from Heaven.
    B. Jesus wanted God to hear him.
    C. Jesus wanted the people to know he was a righteous man.

4 Just as God created life in the beginning by speaking, so Jesus was able to restore life at his command.
    ❑ True   ❑ False

5 HELL

1. The rich man went to _____ because he ignored God and lived only for himself. There are no _____ chances in Hell to gain Heaven. _____ can only be received if one _____ and believes during this lifetime.

second	Hell	repents	Mercy

2. The Scripture says that if man refuses to believe God's written Word, then he will not be convinced even if someone is raised from the dead.
    ❑ True   ❑ False

6 ACCEPTANCE AND BETRAYAL

1. When Jesus rode into Jerusalem on a colt, the enthusiastic crowd responded with applause and praise, hoping he would overthrow their Roman oppressors. They were unaware that in doing so, they were:
    A. fulfilling a 500 year-old prophecy given by the Prophet Zechariah.
    B. doing exactly what their rivals wanted them to do.

2. Because of Jesus' popularity among the huge Passover crowds, the religious leaders were:
    A. planning to kill him publicly as an example.
    B. hoping Jesus would perform another miracle.
    C. afraid to kill Jesus.
    D. wanting to make Jesus king.

3. Jesus said that the Passover loaf represented his [body / friendship].

4. Drinking of the cup was symbolic of how Jesus' blood would soon be poured out for many people.
   ❑ True   ❑ False

CHAPTER THIRTEEN

REVIEW QUESTIONS

1 THE GARDEN

1. Because Jesus submitted his human will to that of his heavenly Father, he had no problem thinking about the suffering he was about to experience.
   ❑ True   ❑ False

2. When the mob, sent to arrest Jesus, told him who they were looking for, Jesus acknowledged who he was with an emphatic "I AM!" A literal translation of the original language would be:
   A. "I AM in control."
   B. "I AM, right now, God."
   C. "I AM stronger than this mob."

3. In reaction to Jesus identifying himself as "I AM,"
   A. the crowd jeered.
   B. Judas Iscariot scoffed.
   C. the crowd fell backward to the ground.

4. When Jesus was arrested, Peter, in an effort to protect him, cut off a servant's ear. In response, Jesus healed the man's ear—showing compassion even in the midst of turmoil.
   ❑ True   ❑ False

5. When the high priest asked Jesus, "Are you THE PROMISED MESSIAH?" Jesus answered, ["I am" / "I am not"].

2 THE PLACE OF THE SKULL

1. The Sanhedrin found Jesus guilty on two charges but only one was true:
   A. he claimed to be Christ / the Messiah.
   B. he forbid payment of taxes to Caesar.

2. As a king, Jesus had political ambitions. He wanted to begin his reign in Jerusalem.
   ❑ True   ❑ False

3. Neither Herod nor Pilate could find Jesus guilty of anything deserving the death penalty.
   ❑ True   ❑ False

4. The prophet David wrote about the Messiah's crucifixion _____ before it became Rome's official form of capital punishment.

200 years	800 years	50 years

5. Jesus assured the thief on the cross next to him that he would go to Paradise, because he was putting his [*wish / trust*] in Jesus to deliver him from the consequences of sin.

6. When Jesus died, the Temple curtain in front of the Holy of Holies was torn from top to bottom. This was significant because:
   A. to look behind the curtain was to die.
   B. the high priest had said such an event would happen.
   C. only God could have torn the thick curtain. It was impossible for man to do so.

7. The Greek word translated, *"It is finished,"* had several different usages during the time of Christ. Which of the following accurately expresses its meaning (Mark three)?
   A. The job you gave me is finished.
   B. The debt is finished.
   C. My life is done.
   D. The search for an acceptable sacrifice is finished.

8. The day Jesus died was the climax of the Passover week—the day when the lamb was killed.
   ❑ True   ❑ False

9. A Roman soldier thrust a spear into Jesus' chest but wasn't certain that Jesus was dead.
   ❑ True   ❑ False

3 The Empty Tomb

1. The tomb was very secure because (Mark two):
   A. the disciples spent the night in front of the tomb.
   B. it was guarded by well-trained soldiers.
   C. the entrance to the tomb was sealed.

2. When the angel of the Lord appeared in front of the tomb, the guards initially:
   A. passed out—overcome with fear.
   B. ran away in terror.
   C. fought the angel.

3. The angel told Mary and Salome that Jesus was:
   A. sleeping.   B. alive—risen from the dead.   C. dead.

4. The Scripture says that when John saw the empty tomb, he:
   A. fled.   B. wept.
   C. believed.   D. panicked.

5. Jesus, THE ANOINTED ONE, had crushed Satan's [head / heel], just as God had promised back in the Garden of Eden.

6. Death is the result of sin. Jesus did not have to die because he was sinless. He died willingly.
   ❑ True   ❑ False

CHAPTER FOURTEEN

REVIEW QUESTIONS

1 THE STRANGER

1. Jesus explained to the two men that Christ had to _____ (Mark three).

   | suffer | die | resurrect | reincarnate |

2. Jesus used _____ to explain all the events surrounding his death, burial and resurrection.
   A. the Jewish Scriptures
   B. a parable
   C. history books

2 THE LAW AND THE PROPHETS
—ADAM TO NOAH—

1. God created man [with a will / without emotions] so that by his obedient choices, he would honour God.

2. Match the phrases below. According to the Word of God, everyone faces three types of death:

___ A. Death of the body

___ B. Death of a relationship

___ C. The Second Death

1. God separated from mankind.

2. the spirit separated from the body.

3. separated forever from God and all future joy by being confined forever in the Lake of Fire.

3. No one can make himself acceptable to God.
   ❑ True   ❑ False

4. Match the following phrases to form complete sentences.

___ A. Just as an animal died to clothe Adam and Eve in *acceptable* clothing,

___ B. Just as Abel brought a *blood sacrifice* to gain forgiveness for sin,

___ C. Just as there was only *one* ark and *only* one door to safety,

___ D. Man cannot *reach* or please God through any religious effort,

___ E. Just as the people of Noah's day were *judged* for their sins,

1. so God will *judge* all men, regardless of their philosophy of life.

2. so Jesus died to make us *acceptable* in the presence of God.

3. but God *reached* down to man in the person of Jesus Christ.

4. so Jesus is the *only* way to eternal life.

5. so Jesus became the ultimate *blood sacrifice*, dying so that our sin might be forgiven.

5. Although we were born into this world as enemies of God, because of what Jesus did on the cross we can now be friends.
   ❑ True   ❑ False

6. Every person faces death as a consequence of his personal sin. But God also loves mankind so in his [*mercy / leniency*], he showed man grace. He provided [*work / a way*] for a person to escape that death through [*prayer / Jesus Christ*].

3 THE LAW AND THE PROPHETS
—ABRAHAM TO THE LAW—

1. Match the following phrases to make complete sentences.

____ A. Just as Abraham's son was bound and could not save himself,

____ B. Just as the ram died in Isaac's place,

____ C. Just as Abraham's sin-debt was paid when he trusted God,

1. so Jesus paid our *sin-debt* when we put our trust in him.

2. so Jesus died in our *place* and took our punishment on the cross. He is our substitute.

3. so we are bound by sin and helpless to *save* ourselves from its consequences.

2. Jesus died in our place and took our punishment for sin. He is our [*substitute / equal*].

3. Jesus cried, "It is finished," because he had done his part in paying our sin-debt. Now we need to do our part in paying for our sin-debt.
   ❑ True   ❑ False

4. God credited righteousness to Abraham's *Certificate of Debt* because he was looking ahead to what Jesus would do on the cross.
   ❑ True   ❑ False

5. Which of the following statements are true in relation to the word *believe*?
   A. It is synonymous with *trust, confidence* and *faith.*
   B. It is built on fact.
   C. It involves mental assent and heart trust.

6. Match the comparisons between the Passover and Jesus:

____ A. The Passover lamb had to be *perfect*.

____ B. The lamb had to be a *male*.

____ C. The lamb died in the *place* of the firstborn.

____ D. The Israelites were not to break any *bones* of the Passover lamb.

____ E. When the angel of death came, he would *pass over* the house that had the blood applied.

1. None of Jesus' *bones* were broken.

2. Jesus was *sinless*.

3. God provided a way for his judgment on sin to *pass over* us. Instead the judgment came to rest on Jesus on the cross.

4. Jesus died in our *place*, as our substitute.

5. Jesus was a *man*.

7. Jesus, the *Lamb of God,* was crucified on the same day the *Passover lamb* was killed. He died at the hour the evening sacrifice was offered in the Temple.
   ❑ True   ❑ False

8. Keeping the Ten Commandments helps us restore the broken relationship with God.
   ❑ True   ❑ False

9. Jesus had no sin of his own to die for, so he was able to die for the sins of the whole world.
   ❑ True   ❑ False

10. When we are clothed in the righteousness of Christ, in God's eyes we have a *righteousness that is* <u>*equal*</u> *to God's holiness.*
    ❑ True   ❑ False

11. God says we are justified. We are [*sinless / declared righteous*].

12. We can only be *found righteous* by God if we put our _____ in the fact that Jesus died on the cross in our place.

    | wishes   faith   efforts |

4 THE LAW AND THE PROPHETS
—THE TENT TO THE BRONZE SERPENT—

1 Match the following phrases to make complete sentences.

The sacrifice was to be …   **Jesus …**

___ A. from the *herd* or *flock.*   1. is *sinless.*

___ B. a *male.*   2. died in our *place.*

___ C. without *defect.*   3. is the *Lamb* of God.

___ D. accepted in man's *place.*   4. is a *male.*

___ E. an *atonement-covering* for man's sin.   5. was the *blood sacrifice* made for us.

___ F. a *blood sacrifice.*   6. is our way to have *forgiveness* of sin.

2. Match the following Scripture verses regarding Jesus with the parallel item in the Tabernacle:

___ A. *"I am the way, the truth, and the life. No one can come to the Father except through me."* JOHN 14:6 NLT

    1. The Lampstand

___ B. *"I am the Light of the world; he who follows Me will not walk in the darkness, but will have the Light of life."* JOHN 8:12 NASB

    2. The Table of Bread

___ C. *"Truly... I say to you, he who believes has eternal life. I am the bread of life."* JOHN 6:47,48 NASB

    3. The Atonement-Cover

___ D. *"Their sins and lawless acts I will remember no more." And where these have been forgiven, there is no longer any sacrifice for sin.* HEBREWS 10:17-18 NIV

    4. The one Gate

3. God's Word says that when a person believes, he is adopted into God's family with the full rights of a son. Instead of being *estranged*, he becomes a son.

    ❑ True   ❑ False

4. The animal sacrifice was a temporary payment for sin, but Jesus was the permanent and final Lamb.

    ❑ True   ❑ False

5. Match the following comparisons with Jesus:

___ A. Just as the Bronze Altar was the *first step* to God through the blood sacrifice,

___ B. Just as the Israelite who brought an animal sacrifice was showing *faith* in God's instructions,

___ C. Just as the Tabernacle curtain separating man from God was torn in half, giving man *entrance* into the Holy of Holies,

___ D. Just as the only way for the Israelites to be healed from their snake bites was to simply *turn and look* at the bronze serpent,

1. so Jesus, our substitute Lamb, is the *first* and *only step* to having a right relationship with God.

2. so God sent Jesus to suffer as a sacrifice for man so that we might *enter* boldly into God's presence.

3. so we must put our *trust* in what Jesus did on the cross.

4. so the only way we can become right with God is to repent by simply *turning and looking* in faith to Jesus, believing that he paid our sin-debt.

6. Just as Jesus rose from the grave, conquering death, so we become spiritually alive, now and for all eternity.

   ❏ True   ❏ False

7. Although man was once spiritually dead and facing eternal death in the Lake of Fire, those who believe are now spiritually alive and will dwell forever in __ __ __ __ __ __ with their Creator.

5 THE LAW AND THE PROPHETS
—JOHN TO THE RESURRECTION—

1. Choosing to go our own way, we are lost and estranged from God because of our sin.

   ❏ True   ❏ False

2. Match the following phrases to make complete sentences:

   ___ A. Just as a shepherd searches for and rescues his lost sheep,

   ___ B. Just as a slave was chained, helpless to deliver himself,

   ___ C. Just as there was only one door to a sheep pen,

   ___ D. Just as the Pharisees could not reach God through keeping the Ten Commandments,

   1. so we are slaves to Satan and helpless to save ourselves.

   2. so we cannot reach God through good works or deeds.

   3. so Jesus left Heaven and died on the cross for us, in our place, to pay our sin-debt in order to rescue us from death.

   4. so there is only one way to God.

3. Circle two reasons why Jesus died:

   A. Our sin demanded death—separation.

   B. Jesus had to die for his own sin.

   C. Jesus took the eternal consequences of our sin—and those of the world—upon himself.

4. On the cross there was a great exchange. Jesus took our _____ and gave us his _____.

   | faith | sin | confidence | righteousness | love |

5. Who is responsible for the death of Jesus on the cross?
   A. Only the Roman soldiers
   B. The religious leaders
   C. The whole world including every person who has or will ever live

6. The resurrection showed that Jesus had victory over __ __ __ __ __; he had removed its terrible finality.

7. The Word of God clearly states that eternal life is a:
   A. gift (something undeserved, free).
   B. reward (something merited).
   C. wage (something earned).

8. It is not the size of our faith, but in *whom* we are placing our faith that is significant.
   ❑ True   ❑ False

9. By __ __ __ __ __ ,

   we *believe* that Jesus died in our place for our sin.

   we *believe* that Jesus paid our sin-debt.

   we *believe* that God's justice was satisfied by Jesus' death.

   we *believe* that God gives us the gift of eternal life.

CHAPTER FIFTEEN

REVIEW QUESTIONS

1 ALL THAT THE PROPHETS HAVE SPOKEN

1. Over 700 years before the birth of Jesus, the Prophet Isaiah wrote a vivid description of the Messiah's sufferings.
   ❑ True   ❑ False

2. Though hundreds of specific prophecies were fulfilled in the life of Jesus, the disciples were still slow to believe *"all that the prophets have spoken."* Jesus said that they were foolish not to believe.
   ❑ True   ❑ False

2 JESUS RETURNS TO HEAVEN

1. Not long after Jesus' resurrection, he led his disciples out to a hillside and there he disappeared out of their sight into Heaven.
   ❏ True   ❏ False

2. The Word of God declares that Jesus is coming a second time. We can be sure that this will happen because God always keeps his promises.
   ❏ True   ❏ False

3 DO YOU BELIEVE THE PROPHETS?

1. According to the Scriptures, God in his grace will tolerate sin for a while, but then in his justice he will judge it—either in this life or after death.
   ❏ True   ❏ False

2. After hearing the message about Jesus from Paul, Felix said he wanted to wait for a more convenient time.
   ❏ True   ❏ False

3. Saul, Herod Agrippa, Agrippa II, Felix—all these men made a choice. It's the same choice we face.
   ❏ True   ❏ False

ANSWERS FOR
CHAPTER ONE

1 Prologue

No questions

2 Getting Things Straight

<table>
<tr><td>1. True</td><td>page 10</td></tr>
<tr><td>2. True</td><td>page 10</td></tr>
<tr><td>3. E</td><td>pages 10-12</td></tr>
</table>

3 A Unique Book

<table>
<tr><td>1. B, C, D</td><td>pages 12-13</td></tr>
<tr><td>2. True</td><td>page 13</td></tr>
<tr><td>3. B</td><td>page 13</td></tr>
<tr><td>4. A</td><td>page 13</td></tr>
<tr><td>5. False. It is true that God guided the prophets and what was recorded was precisely what he wanted written but these men were not free to add their own private thoughts.</td><td>page 14</td></tr>
<tr><td>6. C</td><td>page 15</td></tr>
<tr><td>7. True</td><td>page 15</td></tr>
<tr><td>8. False. The prophets themselves testified that God would preserve his written Word in such a way that it would never change.</td><td>page 15</td></tr>
<tr><td>9. True</td><td>page 15</td></tr>
<tr><td>10. B</td><td>page 16</td></tr>
</table>

ANSWERS FOR
CHAPTER TWO

1 In the Beginning God ...

<table>
<tr><td>1. False. The Scripture states that God had no beginning and will have no end—he is eternal.</td><td>page 19</td></tr>
<tr><td>2. everlasting or eternal</td><td>page 19</td></tr>
<tr><td>3. C</td><td>page 22</td></tr>
<tr><td>4. I Am</td><td>page 22</td></tr>
<tr><td>5. True</td><td>page 22</td></tr>
<tr><td>6. False. God alone is the Most High. He is ruler over everything—all that we see and don't see.</td><td>pages 22</td></tr>
<tr><td>7. A</td><td>page 23</td></tr>
<tr><td>8. B</td><td>page 23</td></tr>
</table>

Find the answers on these pages in the book

2 ANGELS, HOSTS, AND STARS

1. A, B
2. True
3. creates, owns
4. A, C
5. C
6. worth

page 24
page 24
page 25
page 26
page 26
page 26

ANSWERS FOR
CHAPTER THREE

1 HEAVEN AND EARTH

1. True
2. B, C
3. True
4. False. God not only knows and understands everything, he is also all-powerful.
5. True

page 29
pages 29, 31
page 29

page 29
page 30

2 IT WAS GOOD

1. False. According to the Scripture, God created all of the universe, including our world, in six days.
2. True
3. order
4. True
5. A, B, C
6. A
7. loving, caring

pages 29-44
page 34
page 35
page 36
page 37
page 37
page 38

3 MAN AND WOMAN

1. False. Rather, man is like a mirror that reflects the image but is not the object itself.
2. C
3. False. As Creator of Adam and Eve, they belonged to him. He was their Owner and knew what was best for them.
4. B
5. choose, obey
6. True
7. True
8. True

page 39
page 40

page 41
page 42
page 42
page 43
page 43
page 43

ANSWERS FOR
CHAPTER FOUR

1 SATAN

1.	pride	page 50
2.	C	page 50
3.	sin	page 50
4.	A: b, c B: a, d	page 51

2 HAS GOD SAID?

1.	A	page 52
2.	B	page 54
3.	True	page 55
4.	guilt	page 56
5.	True	page 56
6.	choice; sin	page 57
7.	False. God is holy and therefore cannot tolerate sin in his presence. Adam and Eve's disobedience opened a vast gulf in the relationship between God and man.	page 57
8.	False. God considers all disobedience to be sin.	page 57

3 WHERE ARE YOU?

1.	True	page 58
2.	A, C	page 59
3.	B	pages 59-60
4.	True	page 60
5.	A	page 60
6.	True	page 60
7.	B	page 61
8.	death	page 61

4 DEATH

1.	False. Death never means annihilation or non-existence in Scripture.	page 62
2.	wages	page 62
3.	A: 3 B: 1 C: 2	pages 62-65
4.	True	page 63
5.	Lake of Fire	page 64
6.	second	page 64
7.	True	page 66

ANSWERS FOR
CHAPTER FIVE

1 A PARADOX
1. laws — page 69
2. D — page 69
3. True — page 69
4. sin, perfection — pages 69-70
5. True — page 71
6. False. Because man was a sinner, he did not deserve God's love, grace and mercy. — page 72
7. all — page 73
8. A — page 73
9. C — page 73

2 ATONEMENT
1. remove — page 74
2. death — page 74
3. False. Cain and Abel inherited Adam's sin nature. — page 75
4. B — page 75
5. substitute — page 76
6. A, C — page 76
7. B, C, D — page 77
8. accepted — page 78
9. A, D, E — pages 80-81

3 THE PROPHET ENOCH
1. True — page 82
2. A, C — page 82

4 THE PROPHET NOAH
1. B — page 84
2. True — page 84
3. B, C — page 84
4. death — page 84
5. False. Unlike man who sometimes threatens but never delivers, God always keeps his Word. — page 86
6. True — page 87

5 BABEL
1. C — page 91
2. False. The Scripture says that God is the only one worthy to have his name exalted. — pages 91-92

ANSWERS FOR
CHAPTER SIX

1 THE PROPHET JOB

2 THE PROPHET ABRAHAM

3 GENUINE BELIEF

4 HAGAR AND ISHMAEL

5 ISHMAEL AND ISAAC

6 THE PROVIDER

ANSWERS FOR
CHAPTER SEVEN

1 JACOB AND JUDAH

1. A
2. Deliverer

page 111
page 111

2 THE PROPHET MOSES

1. B
2. C

pages 113-114
page 114

3 PHARAOH AND THE PASSOVER

1. A, B
2. way
3. False. God gave specific instructions to the Israelites and made it clear that they were to be obeyed.
4. True
5. True
6. A: 3   B: 1   C: 2

page 116
pages 117-118

page 119
pages 119-120
page 120
page 120

ANSWERS FOR
CHAPTER EIGHT

1 BREAD, QUAIL AND WATER

1. False. They grumbled and complained.
2. B
3. True

pages 123-124
page 124
page 125

2 TEN RULES

1. C
2. True
3. B
4. True
5. murder
6. True
7. A
8. lies
9. False. God's expectations have remained constant and unchanging.
10. True

page 127
page 128
page 128
page 129
page 130
page 130
pages 130-131
page 131

page 131
page 131

3 THE COURTROOM

1. C — page 132
2. True — page 133
3. False. We are incapable of keeping the law consistently and perfectly. — page 133
4. A, B — page 133-134
5. sin — page 134
6. B — page 135
7. A — page 135
8. C — page 135
9. True — page 137

ANSWERS FOR
CHAPTER NINE

1 THE TENT OF MEETING

1. B — page 139
2. A, D — page 140
3. False. The Israelites were to construct the Tabernacle precisely according to the pattern God had given them. — page 140
4. B — page 140
5. True — page 144
6. False. Upon entering the Tabernacle courtyard, man's first step to approaching God was to offer a sacrifice on the Bronze Altar. — page 145
7. hand, head, die, substitute, accepted — page 146
8. C — page 146
9. True — page 147
10. blood, Day of Atonement — page 147

2 UNBELIEF

1. accountable — page 149
2. True — page 149
3. False. God's purpose in judgment is to bring about a change of attitude described by the word repentance. — page 149
4. C — page 149
5. True — page 149
6. death — page 150

3 JUDGES, KINGS AND PROPHETS

1. False. God wants all people of all nations to trust in him alone. — page 151
2. B — page 152
3. A, C — pages 152-153
4. C — page 155
5. B — page 156
6. True — page 157

ANSWERS FOR
CHAPTER TEN

1 THE ANGEL GABRIEL

1. True — page 161
2. A — page 162
3. True — page 164
4. B, C — page 166
5. False. THE PROMISED DELIVERER was the Lord Almighty come to earth as the baby Jesus. — page 167

2 THE MESSIAH

1. A: 3 B: 1 C: 2 D: 4 — pages 168-170
2. A, C — page 172
3. B — page 174
4. True — page 174

3 AMONG THE SAGES

1. True — page 175
2. True — page 176

4 THE PROPHET JOHN

1. identification — page 178
2. True — page 178
3. False. To the contrary, these religious leaders were proud and viewed themselves as better than everyone else. Even though they imposed strict rules on others, they didn't practice what they preached. They needed to change the way they were thinking about their standing before God. — page 178
4. Lamb, before — page 179
5. True — page 180
6. an infinite, finite — page 182

ANSWERS FOR
CHAPTER ELEVEN

1 Tempted

1. True — page 185
2. B — page 185
3. C — pages 185-186
4. False. Jesus said man's primary concern should be his spiritual well-being. — page 185
5. False. Satan always misquotes Scripture, distorting its meaning. — page 186
6. True — page 186
7. False. Jesus, the Creator God, is far more powerful than Satan, a created being. — page 187
8. A — page 187

2 Power and Fame

1. True — page 188
2. False. Jesus was God and gave his words credibility through his actions. — page 188
3. B, C, D — page 189

3 Nicodemus

1. False. He was referring to a spiritual birth. — page 190
2. eternal — page 191
3. C — page 191
4. object — page 191
5. B — page 191
6. True — pages 191-192
7. False. There is no middle ground. Jesus said that if one believes in him, he has eternal life; if not, he already stands condemned. — page 192
8. False. Jesus clearly stated that we can know our future destiny now. — page 192

4 Rejection

1. faith — page 193
2. A, B, C — pages 193-194
3. helplessness, sinfulness — page 195
4. False. None of the disciples were religious leaders. — page 196

5 The Bread of Life

1. A, B — page 198
2. C — page 198

ANSWERS FOR
CHAPTER TWELVE

1 Filthy Rags

1. True — page 201
2. A — page 201
3. humility — page 202
4. A, C, D — page 202
5. False. The Scripture is clear that good deeds cannot earn a right standing with God. — page 202
6. B — page 202
7. True — page 203
8. nothing — page 203

2 The Way

1. True — pages 204-205
2. B — page 205
3. Jesus — page 205
4. way, truth, eternal life — page 205

3 The Plan

1. True — page 205
2. C — page 205
3. False. Jesus immediately rebuked Peter. Not understanding God's plan, Peter was playing into Satan's hands. — page 206
4. True — page 206

4 Lazarus

1. False. Even though we don't know what Martha expected Jesus to do, her faith in him was well-founded. She was convinced that Jesus was the promised Messiah. — page 208
2. True — page 208
3. A — page 209
4. True — page 210

5 Hell

1. Hell, second, Mercy, repents — page 211
2. True — page 212

6 Acceptance and Betrayal

1. A — page 213
2. C — page 213
3. body — pages 214-215
4. True — page 215

ANSWERS FOR
CHAPTER THIRTEEN

1 The Garden

1. False. Though Jesus submitted his human will to that of his heavenly Father, he agonized over the suffering he was about to face. — page 217
2. B — page 217
3. C — page 217
4. True — page 218
5. I am — page 219

2 The Place of the Skull

1. A — page 220
2. False. Though a King, Jesus had no political ambitions. His reign began in the hearts of people. — page 220
3. True — page 223
4. 800 years — page 226
5. trust — page 228
6. A, C — pages 228-229
7. A, B, D — page 230
8. True — page 230
9. False. These soldiers were trained in the art of killing. To bungle a public execution was unthinkable. — page 231

3 The Empty Tomb

1. B, C — page 232
2. A — page 233
3. B — page 233
4. C — page 234
5. head — page 236
6. True — pages 236-237

ANSWERS FOR
CHAPTER FOURTEEN

1 THE STRANGER
1. suffer, die, resurrect — page 239
2. A — pages 239-240

2 THE LAW AND THE PROPHETS
—ADAM TO NOAH—
1. with a will — page 241
2. A: 2 B: 1 C: 3 — page 242
3. True — page 243
4. A: 2 B: 5 C: 4 D: 3 E: 1 — pages 243-246
5. True — page 245
6. mercy, a way, Jesus Christ — page 246

3 THE LAW AND THE PROPHETS
—ABRAHAM TO THE LAW—
1. A: 3 B: 2 C: 1 — pages 247-248
2. substitute — page 247
3. False. Jesus' death completely paid man's sin-debt—past, present and future. — page 248
4. True — page 248
5. A, B, C — pages 248-249
6. A: 2 B: 5 C: 4 D: 1 E: 3 — pages 249-250
7. True — page 250
8. False. The Ten Commands show us that we are sinners who can only come to God in God's way. — page 251
9. True — pages 252-253
10. True — page 253
11. declared righteous — page 253
12. faith — page 253

4 THE LAW AND THE PROPHETS
—THE TENT TO THE BRAZEN SERPENT—
1. A: 3 B: 4 C: 1 D: 2 E: 6 F: 5 — page 255
2. A: 4 B: 1 C: 2 D: 3 — pages 255-257
3. True — page 257
4. True — pages 257-258
5. A: 1 B: 3 C: 2 D: 4 — pages 255-259
6. True — page 259
7. Heaven — page 259

5 THE LAW AND THE PROPHETS
—JOHN TO THE RESURRECTION—

1. True   page 259
2. A: 3   B: 1   C: 4   D: 2   pages 259-263
3. A, C   page 260
4. sin, righteousness   page 261
5. C   page 261
6. death   page 262
7. A   page 264
8. True   page 264
9. faith   page 264

ANSWERS FOR
CHAPTER FIFTEEN

1 ALL THAT THE PROPHETS HAVE SPOKEN

1. True   page 267
2. True   pages 267-268

2 JESUS RETURNS TO HEAVEN

1. True   page 268
2. True   page 268

3 DO YOU BELIEVE THE PROPHETS?

1. True   page 270
2. True   page 271
3. True   page 271

GoodSeed® International
P. O. Box 3704
Olds, AB T4H 1P5
CANADA
Business: 403 556-9955
Facsimile: 403 556-9950
Email: info@goodseed.com

GoodSeed Australia
1800 897-333
info.au@goodseed.com

GoodSeed Canada
800 442-7333
info.ca@goodseed.com

BonneSemence Canada
Service en français
888 314-3623
info.qc@goodseed.com

GoodSeed Europe
info.eu@goodseed.com

GoodSeed UK
0800 073-6340
info.uk@goodseed.com

GoodSeed USA
888 654-7333
info.us@goodseed.com

www.goodseed.com

GoodSeed® International is a not-for-profit organization that exists for the purpose of clearly communicating the contents of this book in this language and others. We invite you to contact us if you are interested in ongoing projects or translations.